Fledge

Jonathan Humble

Maytree Press 2020

Published 2020 by Maytree Press

www.maytreepress.co.uk

ISBN: 978-1-913508-07-4

A CIP catalogue record of this book is available from the
British Library.

Cover image: Edgelands by Suzi Thompson

Maytree 018

Printed in the UK by PiggyPrint

Acknowledgements

Thank you to the editors of the following publications where earlier versions of some of the poems in *Fledge* first saw the light of day ...

The Poetry Village (David Coldwell); Obsessed With Pipework (Charles Johnson and Katerina Neocleous); Clear Poetry (Ben Banyard); Numenius Press (Karen Lloyd); Atrium Poetry (Holly Magill and Claire Walker); Riggwelter (Jonathan Kinsman); Zoomorphic (Susan Richardson); Amaryllis (Stephen Daniels); Fair Acre Press (Nadia Kingsley); Burning House Press (guest editor Amee Nassrene Broumand); Barren Magazine (Jason D. Ramsey); Handstand Press (Kerry Darbishire, Kim Moore and Liz Nuttall); Bonnie's Crew (Kate Garrett); The Blue Nib (Tracy Gaughan).

About the Author

Jonathan Humble was born in the Port of Goole. He works as a deputy head teacher in Cumbria and has taught in primary schools for thirty-six years. He trained in the power industry as a student engineer in East Yorkshire, worked as a lettuce picker for East Coast Salads and as a painter in a corrugated card factory. His poems have appeared in a number of anthologies and other publications online and in print. A collection of his light verse, *My Camel's Name Is Brian*, was published in 2015 by TMB Books and his poems for children have been shortlisted for the Caterpillar Poetry Prize and the York Mix Poetry Competition. He reads regularly at poetry events in Cumbria and Lancashire and has delivered poetry workshops in schools for The Wordsworth Trust.

For Fiona …

*A trust in truth is not weighed as cost
and light in ragged leaves endures.
Though slight,
as scythes descend and sweep the dream,
it will not fail at dusk.*

Dandelion Sun

Contents

Dandelion Sun

A child's sun finds a dream in young eyes.
In blinks of dandelion eclipses,
refracted light reflects on retinas
holding warmth in ragged leaves
below a flower standing up and out.

Ryegrass and foxtail for company,
a golden head of petals,
swaying and slight,
is there and gone and there again.

The wings of friends unfold to test the air
with thoughts aloft in stretching skies,
days that lift and soar with matchless views.
They seek what hawks perceive as truth
yet still count the faces that look familiar.

And dipping hands in search of clues,
a box of sights,
of scent and sound,
they choose a shade and wear a skin,
fit in and lose themselves as one of many.

But *this* child blinks dandelion eclipses;
hawkbit tinctures bathing open eyes
with picture sun now placed behind an ear
while looking up and out.

A trust in truth is not weighed as cost
and light in ragged leaves endures.
Though slight,
as scythes descend and sweep the dream,
it will not fail at dusk.

Fledge

Haunting places where secret agents hid,
I return to childhood as a stranger.
All games played for keeps;
no second chances.

Walking with shadows:
a skinned knee congregation of risk takers,
worshipping by abandoned canals,
waist high baptisms in summer filth.

Staring back in black and white,
whoops of unwashed eight year olds,
careless of cars, heroic and helmetless,
tamed old bikes in half-mast socks.

We built dens in fireweed by railway tracks,
unaware of summer weddings and passing poets,
watched over by water towers,
Tom Pudding hoists and dockland cranes;

sentinels which I remember well,
but which do not remember me.

One Called Paul

Five drab juveniles land outside my window;
goth eyeliner, raucous and rucking over territory,
fouling up my window ledge, five floors high.

Under murmuration shadows, three leave suddenly,
startle the two, who, drawing close, look to each other,
before the larger wings it with thousands over late city skies.

The smallest catches reflections in the high rise glass,
checks its rag tag feathers for signs of iridescence
emerging in the half-light of a noisy urban dusk.

But through my window, I see only reluctance in movement.
I wonder if this one's worried; ill-prepared to join in
and just needs a little more time to practise.

Fireweed

Grown wild, unclaimed and loose in lanes,
he peed higher, spat further, swore louder
than any other latchkey street weed.

Green acolytes, summoned with strangled
banshee howls, were drawn in adoration
as he spoke to us in bloodied tongues for a dare.

Envied for knowledge of hidden pathways
by the brick pond and his dead bat in a matchbox,
which some could see for tuppence.

Pursuing the lost, always the first over fences,
through unknown undergrowth, into rank canals,
all consequences ignored in a rush for wheels.

Admired as risk taker, hands free on old bikes,
the world upside down in the canopies of trees,
a body confident in the friction of bare skin.

Solemnly, we'd gift him our bruised fruit,
liberated from the floor of the Saturday market,
consumed when the rhythms of real life paused.

No quarter ever sought or given,
committed to blood and rain and wind and sun.
And though at twelve, his spark burned fierce,

it burned short from dying embers; snuffed out
in a consumptive breeze, warranting five perfunctory
lines of local news and a cheap cremation urn.

Little Rowan

Should I worry, little rowan,
of the dark the solstice brings?

Is my gratitude a weight
and do you fret, you faerie tree?

Born of lightning,
a cracked erratic shocked to life,
you stand with flights of leaves emerging
from the eagle's gift of feathers,
shooting wings of green
from a cold stone cleft.

Are you sad when spring blossoms,
dancing on your runes of wood,
become stained with blood
ordained by ancient gods?

Do your black stars offer protection
under this Samhain moonlight,
as the veil thins and we wait
for our visitors to arrive?

Are you ready, little rowan?

And Yet

Curtains remain drawn, as the day comes with rain
like a returning memory. In darkness, early moments
rest on heavy eyes, closed to a wave of sickness.
In the residue of cracked ashtrays and stale alcohol,
sit diary entries of dissolute nights with succubae;
a debt of bad shillings that smothers and oppresses.

With a switch click of artificial light, a three-quarter
circular tea stain on the old and damaged veneer
of a bedside table screams normality.
But the mundane hides chaos. The dark refocuses,
squats on the body amid the morning's silent rage
and dusty sheets of this year's end chapters.

And yet, the Sun at winter solstice still rises,
to move again at the end of a pendulum swing
towards the promise of late spring's trick of light;
an ache in the chest for remembered summers,
the turbulent sunlit hours of an urban childhood,
anticipating the welcome return of migrant visitors.

Ahead are days when looking out of windows
will be rewarded with scenes of hectic flight,
the freshness of a clear cobalt canvas,
arrowed shrieks slicing through a wintered condition,
lifting the darkness of a season's sadness
and easing the debt so I might breathe again.

Caught In Concrete

Misplaced upstart sycamore,
shooting from damaged concrete.

What drives such green confidence,
sprung as you are from wayward keys,
late buffeted by autumn elements
and the caprice of a council leaf blower?

Flying against reason,
stubbornly mocking the odds and gods
with rude and purposed growth,
some imperative demanding vigour
as if you're earmarked for higher service,
out of reach and unknown
to this observer.

When you become fixed,
will you stop and take breath?
Will you then regret your roots?
Should we consider relocation now,
free from a cemented aggregate
destined to limit lofty plans?

I offer my services, lost tree.

I have a spade.

I know a place.

Just say the word.

Elegy For A Peevish Bee

Temper rising, she becomes a blur of business,
works at glass and frame, vents a blast of angry wings
in search of phantom gaps or phased matter.

Close outside, snapdragons sway encouragingly,
zinnias gesture from plastic boxes beyond the window,
rays of light reflect and raise the stakes.

Frustration takes her; she begins to butt the pane,
anguish as real as the vibrations bounced
off this double-glazed sound board.

But rail as she might against the unseen,
against the barrier between her and home,
she cannot cross this hidden veil to the other side.

And me, I see beyond a peevish bee
my mother leathering the window,
complaining of muck and dust and dry weather.

Leveret

after Carolyn Jess-Cooke

Forty weeks I wondered what would happen.
Bought a tiny cardigan while waiting,
embroidered with some meadow hares in sunshine
and wee blue shoes that you would never wear.

With little witchy hand you grasped my finger,
your body wrapped in heirloom knitted cloth,
each breath I watched and worried in the pauses
and worried as within the sling I held you.

The dandelions spoke your name in secret,
it drifted with the seeds upon a breeze
to leverets that hid among the sweet grass
who saved a place of safety from the foxes.

While in the meadow, hares lay still and quiet,
I walked abroad among a crowd of strangers,
each eye with threat or hidden malice watching,
and as you slept, I'd slay the beasts and dragons.

I walked on broken glass, endured the lightning
and carried you one last time in the autumn,
until with curtains closed amid the silence,
I placed the hares and wee blue shoes in cotton.

Then It Rains

You ask on my behalf to rise and leave,
to dress without the hindrance
of bootlace worms returning at our feet.

In vain, we anticipate permission from spiders,
who watch in shadows, spinning webs
that constrain all action.

Standing, squatting, sitting, we are opposed,
resisted. We are tangled marionettes,
linked with quantum string, each responding
with confused counter movement.

Blink my dears; so many eyes feel the tension
of our unseen bonds. These rainmaker thoughts,
connected across a web of reverberating nonsense
and countless coils, speak to me with jaded explanations;

there are no options again today.
So you tell me that we have to stay and wait.
And I have to listen. So I listen.

Then it rains.

The Safety Of Clouds

On hard wet ground, exposed like a pulsing nerve,
half a yard from the comfort of grass,
it writhed unsteadily to unheard music,
while the connoisseur's eye judged its girth from a bush.

Rainwater marinated and near wasted after a night of passion,
casting tired letter shapes as the sun split clouds overhead,
this six inch nightcrawler knew of its place on the menu,
coelomic fluid spurting in jerked responses
to the half perceived silent threat of a hidden beak.

Meal fixed in a yellow ringed eye,
target acquired, locked on, the beak cared not,
its sudden action initiating a hopeless animated letter S
on the pavement, as the sun denied witness to death throes
and buried itself back in the safety of clouds.

Yew

In search of yew in Borrowdale
that shared the Sun with Judas,
I walk a rutted path,
aware of twinges, snares, rocks,
carrying your paints and easel
along with this bowl of words,
no longer fit for consumption,
mould festering in knots
from sour touching fruit within.
And if these words were berries,
gardeners would stand disappointed
at the canker in the bark below.
And if a perching blackbird,
sang this song from any tree,
on any perfect spring morning,
it would jar, taint the air
and cause the world to frown
at such discordant notes.
We'll find a place to stop, you and I,
and you will paint this landscape,
my eye drawn towards a blemish
where a loose neglected sleeve
was dragged across wet canvas trees
in one careless movement;
a moment you might come to know,
as discarding the bowl by this footpath,
I swallow the words and wait
till the bitter aftertaste subsides,
resolves in time to soil and dust
with Borrowdale's ancient yew.

Invitation To Move On

I am small in the sea, pushed around
by waves that care not for any grain of sand
or stuff that floats in a broken head.

Arms held wide and high, that reach and cling
like a child to a parent when things get rough,
when routines fail and muscles waste.

I hesitate, recoil, cower; skin so thin
these cold water blades could spill these guts
for waiting gulls and wash away this name.

I am caught like the Sun, falling
and hoping to rise again, the horizon watched
from a base of arched feet, soft soles and toes

exposed to the hidden sharpness of shadows.
And though these whispered sea breezes
with caresses would show the way,

for that bastard time waits not for me,
until I learn to surrender, immerse this body,
allow these legs to float and lay back this head,

could I ever take in the whole of the sky?

Adrenaline Junkie

An eye-flash hint of speed
followed by car alarm blackbirds
and I know you've tested the air again;

surfed a low profile wave
in a high stake hawk ride,
navigating marginal branch gaps
and scaring little brown jobs witless,
while beaks from tree and bush
alert the neighbourhood watch.

Standing still, I stay and wait,
late rewarded with an appearance,
stick legs in fluffed up pantaloons,
short stay juvenile power perching on my gate,
a striped waist-coated bully,
Shakespeare's eyas-musket, young eyes wide,
wondering why this foray ended in failure;

no satisfying explosion of feathers
at the end of a breakneck career
through the field by this hedgerow,
planted fifteen years ago in hope of encounters
with feathered adrenaline junkies,
looking for thrills and spills
and old dozy pigeons.

Schrödinger's Mouse

Your love of my raspberries has resulted
in this late evening walk in headtorch,
to hedges of hazel and blackthorn,
far enough from home to foil ideas of return.
Aware of owls ripping through moonlight,
I kneel in damp fescue and sedge,
clutching this tilt trap of quantum uncertainty;
mouse or no mouse? that is the question …

The trap gate opens. You see me for the first time,
holding the moment in beads of black polished glass,
small body wedged, feet splayed, heart racing,
a quiver of tense, anticipating whiskers.
And in that instant, in that brief connection,
my doubts bubble. This is a good deed isn't it?
This forced relocation; got to be a better solution
than back breaking death or slow poisoning.

Although I try to convince myself,
I believe you remain sceptical.
I am your nightmare; the one interrupting
your midnight feasting,
the one separating you from all your
blind, deaf and hairless babies,
the one from which you must flee in terror
the second the black plastic touches the ground.

But, unlike Mr. McGregor, as I stumble one mile
back through darkling woods, soft clart that I am,
I'm hoping the owls have an off day
and secretly, despite your fruit plundering,
I'd quite like to see you again.

Incoming

I am not your enemy dear messenger,
but still your intent feels murderous.

And though your reckless, adrenaline
fuelled passes and doppler cries

have sent these old instincts into full
flight mode, my head disappearing

into my shoulders, my fifty year old
body separated from my bicycle to lie

expediently on this damp grassy bank,
I cannot help but admire your bravery

and the skill with which you missed my
skull by inches. How were you to know,

my crescent beaked nemesis, that I am,
in fact, a fully paid up member of the

RSPB and have no designs on the eggs
you've hidden, but am, instead,

merely on my way back from buying
Morecambe Bay shrimps for my

mother-in-law, who, as well as liking
sea food, agrees with me that

curlews are lovely …

Early Morning Effrontery

I fear porcelain is not your cultural milieu
and your persistence in performing
eight legged running man dances
up sheer white bathroom edifices
under the gaze and malevolence
of the attentive cat bastard
flexing its tail on this toilet seat
will prove an effrontery too far.

Darwin's theory of natural selection
will happen well before adaptation occurs.
Before the hairs on your scopulae
develop greater adhesive powers
and you are able to ascend unharmed,
I suspect you will become terribly broken.

So here I am again, 6:30 in the morning,
offering toilet paper ladders in the bathtub,
before I can shower in peace
and the furry purry assassin,
so beloved in our household,
can be persuaded out of the bathroom
to wander off and find something else
to murder instead.

This Work Is Done

This is an old feeling,
standing by this evening's field,
dark rags hanging, strung on wire,
silent and unmoving under a parched sky.

Which lore or gods apply?
Would it help to free your feathers,
wake thought and memory in cold skulls,
wear a black cape in silhouetted brotherhood?

Should I take up your work?
Am I now a familiar to a Norse god,
with spying eyes in new watching brief,
and become his ears in Midgard?

Should I kneel before the Once and Future King?
Does a messiah hang in this unkindness?
Have I witnessed the end of hope
for an ancient island people?

Should I fly the field, proclaim the news,
take up the role of fate carrier,
become the Mór-Ríoghain's latest messenger
and find a song that sings of coming conflict?

Or is the battle already lost, our colours down,
and what's required this late spring evening is
to take this knapsack, flask and tools
and tell the farmer this work is done?

In Boots Like These

In time spent away,
where horizons are blocked
by walls and traffic and business plans,

where road and high rise
substitute for river course and hill,
and setting out to stretch your legs

you'd also need a head space,
I have to close my eyes to breathe.
In this mind's refuge I'll wear these boots

to get to where I want to be.
I'll stumble over rock and root,
and fray some holes in woolly socks

by Solway's muddied tidal shores,
to Saltom Bay and Silecroft Beach.
I'll imagine days on rutted coastal track,

the kittiwake and Irish Sea for company,
as eager laced, I'll take on routes
from which there'll be no turning back;

those proper walks in boots like these.
I'll push old limestone crag beneath this body;
compel the Silurian world

from Hutton Roof to Cunswick Scar.
I'll work the eyes and feed the heart
with views in Lyth of birds that soar

as cadence clears away
dead weights upon this chest
that drag and snag and catch the throat.

I'll use the rhythms of this mind
where thought and distance coalesce
to fade these binding cares; locked-in despair.

I'll seek clean air by Bassenthwaite,
where rippled clouds reflect in thought
and softened colours move with leaves

the stuff that flows through passing trees.
I'll trek from low to high terrain,
where clearer views perceived as real

reveal such hidden sentinels that raise the skies.
I'll scramble streams in Easdale Ghyll.
I'll plod and push the limits

as fresh rivulets of rain
blend on tired skin with sweat,
pulse synchronised with hard-earned breath,

senses in turmoil becoming clear,
sounds tuned and tempered,
life refocused in revelation,

the world revolving
and this mind made free to feel again.
I'll live and breathe in boots like these.

Still Life

Such a sketchy fox;
broken lines and poor shading,
a child's painting rushed onto paper,
barely recognisable in two dimensions.

Autumn riot of matted fur on frost,
an arrangement set amid a fog of guilt
and quickened wisps of midnight breath.

Deep colour oozes in slow flowing pigment,
warming these shaking hands, melting snow
steaming on the canvas of a hidden kerb.

In the reflected light of a winter moon,
the question, highlighted in a frozen eye,
demands to know which other wretches
feature in this unsolicited tableau;

the shadowed answer stands beside
this painter's composition.

Forty Years On

Walking in snow towards this young ash
triggers memories that surge and well
to overflow as uncontrolled gasps of breath.

This scar deepens with every visit; a vicious erosion,
an abhorrent river coursing down the trunk,
heartwood exposed to light perceived as shameful.

Eyes burn, assaulted by a metre of slashed hate
inflicted on poorly defended and tender bark;
some stranger's loathing of innocence.

Victim and witness to the effects of inadequacy,
I am drawn to repent for assaults by others,
tarred by kith for resurrected screaming deeds.

These clouds know it. These birds are aware.
This tree understands no amount of contrition
could erase the mark of Cain upon its body,

still striving to push blackened buds out
into a world five years after such violence;
still walking with scars forty years on.

Coming Home

I wonder if, like me, these winter skies,
swathed in low cloud above old scars of crag
and frozen garlands of brown bracken,
anticipate the welcome return of African visitors;

if underfoot, limestone bones ache for warmth,
dark fissured slabs buried beneath grass paths,
quietly longing for early May's trick of light,
tired bodies aloft after months of migration.

Do these hazels shiver with the birch and gorse,
recalling dog days, the fall and rise of darts feeding,
the speed of mameluke sabres cutting air curves
with absurd precision over woods in full leaf?

And below, flowing through Kendal's grey canvas,
does the Kent reflect colours of summer expectation,
thoughts of days spent bird watching with you,
on the long return alone to a Cumbrian terrace?

Secrets of Men

Perched on a milestone,
Spy considered offers from fylgjur,
haunting woods like fox wraiths.

Night worn as a cloak, tired bones
aching under breeze ruffled feathers,
his conspiracy betrayed by brother silhouettes
circling in tempered moonlight.

Revealed by flecks of white in beads of jet,
he watched ghost clouds drift like lost leaves,
disturbing stars floating on the edge of eternity,
and looked to his own flight home.

But dawn found him sightless and stiff;
lights extinguished, in shadow of stone,
some fifteen years from his birth
in the boughs of Yggdrasil,
where he'd first told Odin
the secrets of men.

The wings of friends unfold to test the air
with thoughts aloft in stretching skies,
days that lift and soar with matchless views.
They seek what hawks perceive as truth
yet still count the faces that look familiar.

Dandelion Sun